My Feelings

Fabiola Sepulveda

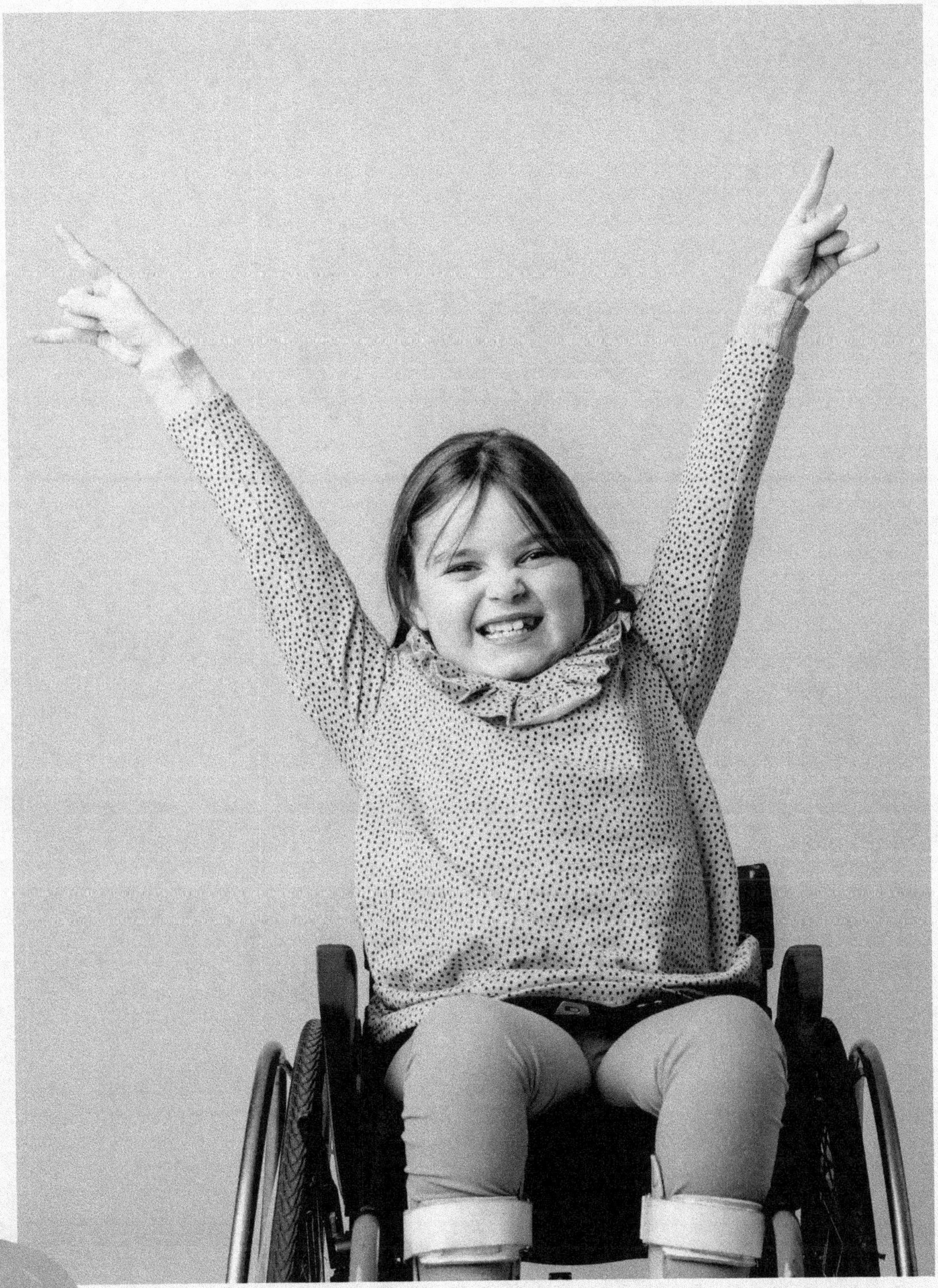

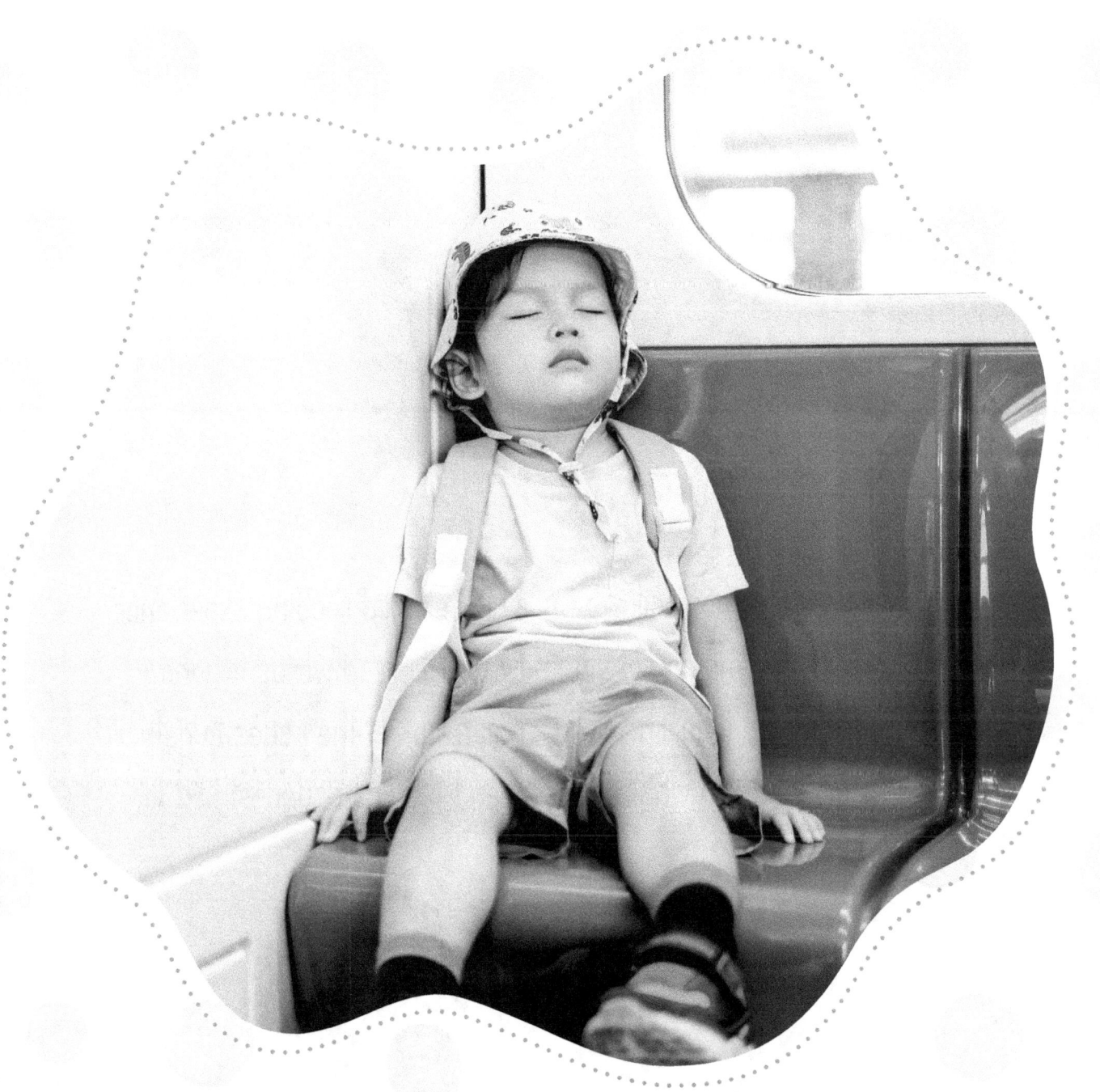

Notes for the Grown-ups

This wordless book allows for a rich shared reading experience for children who do not yet know how to read words or who are beginning to learn. Children can look at the pages to gather information from what they see, and they can suggest text to tell the story.

To extend this reading experience, do one or more of the following:

Ask the child to mirror the expressions in the book. Discuss how our faces can show feelings.

Introduce vocabulary such as these words when looking at the pictures and telling the story you see:

- angry
- bored
- calm
- confused
- disappointed
- embarrassed
- excited

- happy
- hopeful
- lively
- nervous
- playful
- proud
- sad

- scared
- shy
- thoughtful
- tired
- worried

Discuss how we can show emotion with our bodies, using body language. We might cross our arms, look down, skip, fist our hands, and so on.

After reading the pictures, come back to the book again and again. Rereading is an excellent tool for building literacy skills.

Play a guessing game where you and the child each make different facial expressions and guess what emotion you are each showing.

Consultant

Cynthia Malo, M.A.Ed.

Publishing Credits

Rachelle Cracchiolo, M.S.Ed., *Publisher*
Emily R. Smith, M.A.Ed., *SVP of Content Development*
Véronique Bos, *VP of Creative*
Dona Herweck Rice, *Senior Content Manager*

Image Credits: all images from iStock and/or Shutterstock

Library of Congress Cataloging-in-Publication Data

Names: Sepulveda, Fabiola, author.
Title: My feelings / Fabiola Sepulveda.
Description: Huntington Beach, CA : TCM, Teacher Created Materials, [2025]
  | Audience: Ages 3-9 | Summary: "There are so many ways to feel, and we
  feel many different ways each day. How do you feel?"-- Provided by
  publisher.
Identifiers: LCCN 2024003481 (print) | LCCN 2024003482 (ebook) | ISBN
  9798765961124 (paperback) | ISBN 9798765967348 (ebook)
Subjects: LCSH: Emotions in children--Pictorial works--Juvenile literature.
  | Emotions--Pictorial works--Juvenile literature.
Classification: LCC BF723.E6 S47 2025 (print) | LCC BF723.E6 (ebook) |
  DDC 155.4/124--dc23/eng/20240201
LC record available at https://lccn.loc.gov/2024003481
LC ebook record available at https://lccn.loc.gov/2024003482

These or other feeling words can be used to
describe the emotion shown on each page.

page 2: happy	page 12: pleased
page 3: sad	page 13: proud
page 4: angry	page 14: disappointed
page 5: calm	page 15: hopeful
page 6: thoughtful	page 16: playful
page 7: confused	page 17: excited
page 8: shy	page 18: bored
page 9: outgoing	page 19: nervous
page 10: worried	page 20: tired
page 11: scared	page 21: exhausted

Teacher Created Materials

5482 Argosy Avenue
Huntington Beach, CA 92649
www.tcmpub.com
ISBN 979-8-7659-6112-4
© 2024 Teacher Created Materials, Inc.